MILAN
THE CITY AT A GLANCE

Chiesa di San Babila
Located on the site of a temple [...]
the 2nd century, this church, con[...]
by Saint Babila, the Bishop of An[...]
rebuilt at the end of the 11th cent[...]
Piazza San Babila

Golden Triangle
This is where to splash your cash in[...]
the high-end Italian fashion boutiq[...]
that pepper Via Montenapoleone, Via
della Spiga and Via Sant'Andrea.

Torre Velasca
Butting up against the Duomo, this
gorgeously original building pays an
inverted compliment to its medieval
neighbour.
See p011

Palazzo Arcivescovile
Its sophisticated decagonal stable building
and much-imitated 16th-century inner
courtyard make the Archbishop's Palace
worth a visit.
Via dell'Arcivescovado

Duomo
The sheer scale of Milan's 14th-century
cathedral will cause you to pause for
a moment. It seems that big really can
be beautiful.
See p014

Galleria Vittorio Emanuele II
Given a new lease of life by the opening of
chic stores and a hotel under its domed
roof, one of Europe's most elegant shopping
arcades offers plenty of temptation.
See p013

INTRODUCTION
THE CHANGING FACE OF THE URBAN SCENE

Depending on your perspective, Milan is either in the south of the north of Europe, or in the north of the south – making the Milanese, with their proximity to the borders of Switzerland, Austria and France, a different breed from their cousins in the rest of Italy. Milan may not have the history of Rome, the romance of Florence or the beauty of Venice, yet it still attracts scores of international visitors. Many come for its design fairs, such as Milan Fashion Week and the furniture show, the Salone Internazionale del Mobile, held every April. During the latter, the city transforms itself, as every available space is turned into a showroom. These fairs provide a great excuse for a visit, though not if you want a good hotel rate.

Other *ospiti*, as visitors are known, are most likely to be in Milan for the shopping – there's no better place, as the stores are so close together and always sell things that you won't find any-where else. But even that is about to get better with the emergence of the swanky Galleria neighbourhood. Now that Gucci, Tod's and Louis Vuitton have joined Prada (see po86) inside the Galleria Vittorio Emanuele II (see po13) and Valextra (see po85) has opened on Via Alessandro Manzoni, the area is enjoying a luxe renaissance. New hotels – the Park Hyatt (see po20), Straf (see po26) and Town House Galleria (see po36) – not only reinforce this locally, but represent, along with the Bulgari Hotel (see po17), a major and welcome upgrade to the city's hotel scene.

ESSENTIAL INFO
FACTS, FIGURES AND USEFUL ADDRESSES

TOURIST OFFICE
Via Marconi 1
T 02 7252 4301
www.milanoinfotourist.com

TRANSPORT
Car hire
Avis, *T 02 585 8481*
Hertz, *T 02 5858 1312*
Metro
T 800 016 857
www.atm-mi.it
Taxis
Amica Taxi, *T 02 4000*

EMERGENCY SERVICES
Ambulance
T 118
Fire
T 115
Police
T 113
24-hour pharmacy
Stazione Centrale Farmacie
Galleria della Partenze
T 02 669 0935

CONSULATES
British Consulate
Via San Paolo 7
T 02 723 001
www.britain.it
US Consulate
Via Principe Amedeo 2-10
T 02 290 351
www.usembassy.it

MONEY
American Express
Via Larga 4
T 02 721 041
www10.americanexpress.com

POSTAL SERVICES
Post Office
Piazza Cordusio 1
T 02 8791 4446
www.poste.it
Shipping
UPS
T 800 877 877
www.ups.com

BOOKS
Contemporary Italian Product Design
by Silvio San Pietro and Annamaria
Scevola (Edizioni L'Archivolto)
A Farewell to Arms by Ernest
Hemingway (Arrow)
Twilight in Italy by DH Lawrence
(Kessinger Publishing)

WEBSITES
Arts
www.brera.beniculturali.it
www.teatroallascala.org
Design
www.designboom.com
www.gioponti.com
Newspapers
www.corriere.it
www.milandaily.com

COST OF LIVING
**Taxi from Malpensa Airport
to city centre**
€70
Cappuccino
€1.20
Packet of cigarettes
€4
Daily newspaper
€1
Bottle of champagne
€60

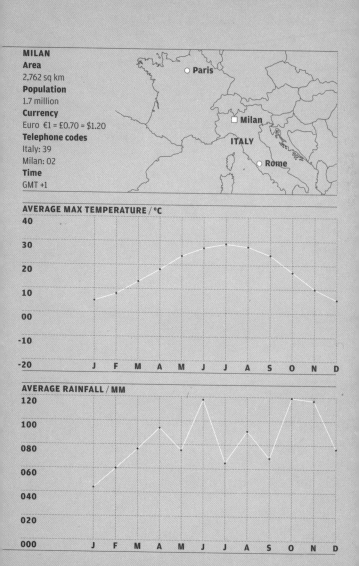

MILAN
Area
2,762 sq km
Population
1.7 million
Currency
Euro €1 = £0.70 = $1.20
Telephone codes
Italy: 39
Milan: 02
Time
GMT +1

Paris

Milan

ITALY

Rome

AVERAGE MAX TEMPERATURE / °C

40											
30											
20											
10											
00											
-10											
-20| J	F	M	A	M	J	J	A	S	O	N	D

AVERAGE RAINFALL / MM

120											
100											
080											
060											
040											
020											
000| J	F	M	A	M	J	J	A	S	O	N	D

NEIGHBOURHOODS

THE AREAS YOU NEED TO KNOW AND WHY

To help you navigate the city, we've chosen the most interesting districts (see the map inside the back cover) and underlined featured venues in colour, according to their location (see below); those venues that are outside these areas are not coloured.

MAGENTA

Starting at the beginning of Corso Magenta with Pasticceria Marchesi, one of Milan's oldest cafés, this area boasts Leonardo da Vinci's famed painting, *The Last Supper*, which is on display in the convent of Santa Maria delle Grazie further along the same *corso*. Milan's chicest neighbourhood also has plenty of fine local shops and our preferred hammam and spa, Habits Culti (see p094), as well as Gio Ponti's Chiesa di San Francesco (see p070).

SEMPIONE

Leading out from the back of Castello Sforzesco is Parco Sempione, which is where you will find Ponti's Torre Branca (see p012), the Milan Triennale, the café/restaurant Coffee Design and the Studio Museo Achille Castiglioni (see p041), in what was once the designer's studio. To the west is Leonardo, one of the city's best cafés, and Cadorna Station, from where you can get the train to Malpensa Airport every 30 minutes.

DUOMO ZONA GALLERIA

Linking Piazza Duomo and Piazza Scala is Galleria Vittorio Emanuele II (see p013), Milan's magnificent shopping arcade. Emerge from its elegant promenades to face the city's arresting late gothic cathedral, the Duomo (see p014). The area is currently undergoing a revival, thanks to the arrival of luxury brands and new hotels opening in and around the Galleria.

GOLDEN TRIANGLE

Milan's famed 'Golden Triangle' of shops is defined by Vie Montenapoleone, Della Spiga and Sant'Andrea. Gucci, Prada, Fendi, Bottega Veneta, Missoni, Armani and Valentino are all here, as is the restaurant Bice, the café Cova and the Four Seasons hotel (see p024). The area has recently opened up to include Vie Verri and San Pietro All'Orto and Corso Venezia, where you'll find Miu Miu and Dolce & Gabbana.

BRERA

The neighbourhood of Brera, which begins just behind La Scala, features many small galleries, concentrated on Via Brera and Via Fiori Chiari, which sell the works of Gio Ponti, Lucio Fontana and Angelo Mangiarotti among others. It is also where you will find the mozzarella bar Obikà on Via Mercato (see p059), Pinacoteca di Brera and Derè, which sells foodstuffs from the best Italian artisan producers.

ZONA TORTONA

During the Salone del Mobile, this area becomes the most important circuit *fuori salone*, 'outside the fair', and is now teeming with the headquarters of big brands such as Giorgio Armani (see the monumental Tadao Ando-designed Teatro Armani, p066). Zona Tortona is also home to the Nhow hotel (see p034) and the Fondazione Arnaldo Pomodoro.

LANDMARKS

THE SHAPE OF THE CITY SKYLINE

Milan's layout can best be described as an historic nucleus around the Duomo (see p014), from which a star-shaped axis of arteries spreads through modern suburbs to the ring road. A few minutes south of Piazza del Duomo, through Piazza Armando Diaz, is Torre Velasca (see p011). To the south-west is the Navigli area, where there are a few remaining canals that once provided irrigation for the Lombardy plains and important trade links between the north and the south of Italy. Here you will also find the Zona Tortona, behind Porto Genova station, a former industrial zone that now boasts numerous design companies and the Nhow hotel (see p034). Another degree or two to the west is Castello Sforzesco (Piazza Castello, T 02 8846 3700), which leads into Parco Sempione, home of the Milan Triennale (Viale Alemagna 6, T 02 724 341) and Gio Ponti's Torre Branca (see p012).

Another exit route from Piazza del Duomo is through the Galleria Vittorio Emanuele II (see p013). From here, head north-west up Via Verdi and you'll arrive in the Brera neighbourhood, which has some excellent galleries. Or from Piazza della Scala take Via Manzoni to arrive at Via Montenapoleone and the entrance to the 'Golden Triangle' of shops and luxury brands. Continue north up Via Manzoni (and then Via Turati) until you find yourself beneath the Pirelli Tower (see p010).

For all addresses, see Resources.

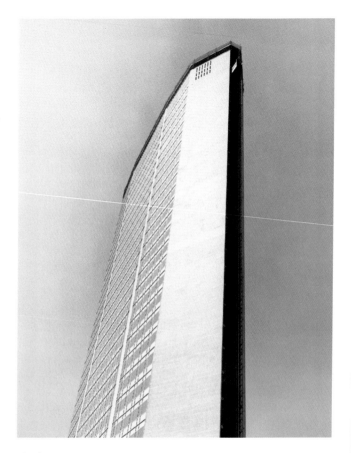

Pirelli Tower

This iconic 32-storey building is proof positive that a modernist skyscraper need not result in repetitive banality. Built for Pirelli, the tyre manufacturer, it was completed in 1959. Its architect, Gio Ponti, was joined by many collaborators on the project, including engineer Pier Luigi Nervi, and the building helped shape Ponti's international reputation and future career. Recently refurbished after a small plane flew into it in 2002, the tower now houses the Lombardy government offices. Apart from visiting the *Pirellone*, as it is fondly referred to by locals, or passing through Piazza Duca d'Aosta en route to or from Central Station, the area around the tower is best avoided.
Piazza Duca d'Aosta 3

Torre Velasca

Much debated at home and abroad at the time of its construction, Torre Velasca was designed in 1957 by BBPR (Gian Luigi Banfi, Ludovico Barbiano di Belgiojoso, Enrico Peressutti and Ernesto Nathan Rogers). A remarkable take on a medieval fortress, it swells on the residential upper storeys, while its cantilevered supports are an inverted nod to the Duomo's famous buttresses (see p014). The lobby is open to the public, but the rest of the building is off-limits, unless you are passing by and feel the need to check the timetable of flights to Mexico City (Mexicana Airlines is on the 15th floor). *Piazza Velasca 5*

Torre Branca

Parco Sempione leads out north-west from Castello Sforzesco (T 02 8846 3700). Towering over the park, next door to the Milan Triennale (T 02 724 341), stands Torre Branca – an elegant 108.6m-high metal tower. It was built by Cesare Chiodi, Ettore Ferrari and Gio Ponti in 1933, as part of an exhibition for the fifth Triennale (at this time, exhibitions were held once every three years, hence the name). If you have a head for heights, climb to the top of the tower and you'll be rewarded with a great view of the city. Torre Branca is open on Wednesday, Saturday and Sunday from April to October.
Viale Luigi Camoen, Parco Sempione,
T 02 331 4120

Galleria Vittorio Emanuele II

Galleria Vittorio Emanuele II was one of the world's first shopping centres. Architect Giuseppe Mengoni's structure was both innovative and daring for its time and has remained hugely influential over the years. Constructed between 1865 and 1878, as two four-storey promenades, with mosaic floors beneath an iron and glass roof, the Galleria swiftly became a fashionable place to shop and a symbol of the belle époque. The Galleria is currently enjoying a renaissance, with several new hotels, including the Town House Galleria (see p036) and several big-name designer stores opening under its domed roof.
Piazza del Duomo/Piazza della Scala

Duomo
Under scaffolding until 2008, Milan's cathedral is one of the largest churches in the world. Commissioned in 1386, by Gian Galeazzo Visconti, it was not completed until the early 1800s (locals joke 1960). A surprisingly elegant mass of marble, more than 100 spires and thousands of statues, it is topped by a gold leaf-covered *Madonnina*.
Piazza del Duomo

HOTELS

WHERE TO STAY AND WHICH ROOMS TO BOOK

In the past few years, Milan's hotel scene has seen some major changes, with the Antonio Citterio-designed Bulgari Hotel (opposite), the jeweller's first venture into hospitality, joining the Park Hyatt (see p020), designed by Ed Tuttle, and its neighbour, the soft-brutalist Straf (see p026), which was designed by Vicenzo di Cotiis. These properties have caused a mini boom in new hotel openings and radically improved the options for the design-savvy traveller. Town House Hotels has recently added a third boutique hotel to its collection, Town House Galleria (see p036), inside the Galleria Vittorio Emanuele II (see p013), while Matteo Thun's Nhow (see p034) is the first hotel to open in Zona Tortona, an area that is always an essential stop-off during both the Salone del Mobile and Milan Fashion Week.

For classic establishments, you can't go wrong with the Four Seasons (see p024) or the Grand Hotel et de Milan (see p032). And two properties that fall into a category all of their own are 3Rooms (see p030), which overlooks the courtyard of the store/gallery/café 10 Corso Como, and Foresteria Monforte (see p035), which has two rooms, one suite and a communal kitchen, where breakfast is served. The latter works best if you come as a group and book all the rooms. The Foresteria offers by far the best- value accommodation in the city.

For all addresses and room rates, see Resources.

Bulgari Hotel

Bulgari opened its first property in 2005 as a joint venture with Ritz Carlton. Designed by Antonio Citterio and partners, the rooms are contemporary in style and superbly fitted out in oak, bronze and matt black marble. Nearly all of the 58 rooms and suites exploit the property's sensational setting overlooking a 4,000 sq m garden which backs onto Milan's Botanical Garden. With such a view, it's hard to believe that you're less than five minutes' walk from Via Montenapoleone. The Bulgari's luxurious spa, gym and pool are the best in the city and, during the summer, the terrace that leads from the bar is the perfect place to meet friends for an *aperitivo*. The Sunday brunch offered is also excellent.

Via Privata Fratelli Gabba 7b, T 02 805 8051, www.bulgarihotels.com

Executive Suite, Bulgari Hotel

Park Hyatt Milan

Designed by Ed Tuttle, who is best known for his work at Amanresorts and The Sukhothai in Bangkok, the Park Hyatt, which opened in October 2003, is just steps from both the Duomo (see p014) and La Scala (T 02 88 791). Housed in a late 19th-century palazzo, the hotel's 117 rooms have generous bathrooms, which occupy around 50 per cent of the room space, while the muted colours, travertine stone and sumptuous fabrics used in the decor create a cool, luxe feel. When it's warm, the tables outside the Park Bar, on one of the few pedestrianised streets in the city, are a great place from which to people watch. Rooms 105 and 205 offer views directly on to the Galleria Vittorio Emanuele II (see p013). As a bonus, you can practically window shop at Prada (see p086) from your bed.

Via Tommaso Grossi 1, T 02 8821 1234, www.milan.park.hyatt.com

Diplomatic Suite Terrace, Park Hyatt

Four Seasons

Since it opened in 1993, the Four Seasons has traditionally been the city's *numero uno* hotel, and it remains extremely popular (during Milan Fashion Week, it is almost impossible to get a room here), despite the more recent competition. Set in what was a 15th-century convent, the best of its 118 rooms surround the magnificent cloistered courtyard (right). If you can, reserve Suite 014, 016, 018 or 019, which are all split-level, or the Cloister Suite 115 (above), which overlooks the courtyard. The service at the Four Seasons is exceptional, and the lobby, where coffee, tea and drinks are served all day, is a great place to spot the city's design and fashion elite, especially during the fair periods. The hotel's central location, nestled in the heart of the shopping district, just adds to its appeal.
Via Gesù 6-8, T 02 77 088,
www.fourseasons.com/milan

Straf

Positioned next to the Galleria (see p013) is the 64-room Straf hotel (short for San Raffaele), designed by Vincenzo de Cotiis. This is the first hotel by the Milan-based architect, whose resumé features a string of retail projects. The hotel's walls, doors and floors are shaped from burnished brass, iron, black stone, scratched glass and cement, and the effect is a kind of soft brutalism, which will appeal to the high quota of design-conscious visitors that Milan attracts. The materials, textures and muted colours used in the decor are all signature de Cotiis. Book a Well-Being Room on the 6th floor, and you will have access to your own private mini spa zone, complete with Japanese auto-massage bed.

Via San Raffaele 3, T 02 805 081,
www.straf.it

3Rooms

When the former journalist Carla Sozzani opened the bar/restaurant/shop/gallery 10 Corso Como in 1991 (think a more sophisticated version of Colette in Paris), it was an instant success. Today, Corso Como is still well worth the pilgrimage, and has single-handedly transformed the once edgy area around Garibaldi Station. The tiny (the clue is in the name) and suitably upmarket bed-and-breakfast operation she opened on the site in 2003 gets a more mixed reception. There is no doubting the elegance of the rooms (right) and the choice of furniture, which is by the likes of Marc Newson and Jean Prouvé, and complemented by state-of-the-art electronics, but it is fair to say that your reception (and indeed your chance of securing a reservation) depend a little too much on who you are.
Corso Como 10, T 02 626 163,
www.3rooms-10corsocomo.com

Grand Hotel et de Milan

With its impressive neo-gothic façade, charming feel and central location on Via Manzoni (at the intersection with Via Montenapoleone), this is the place to stay if you want to be in a grand old hotel. Traditionally favoured by the opera-loving set (Giuseppe Verdi lived here for 20 years until his death in 1901, and Maria Callas made it her home while performing at La Scala), its rooms are either 18th century, Liberty or art deco in style, so it is a good idea to visit the website to choose your favoured decor before booking. We preferred Jerry's Bar before its recent refit (when it was called The Falstaff), but despite their trendy new chocolate-brown aprons, the Grand's *baristas* still mix a great Bellini.
Via Alessandro Manzoni 29, T 02 723 141, www.grandhoteletdemilan.it

Nhow

Located in the area now known as Zona Tortona, which was once full of factories and is now full of design headquarters, Nhow is housed in a former General Electric building. Boasting 249 rooms, including chic standard doubles (above), it was designed by architect Matteo Thun (who also created the Vigilius Mountain Resort in South Tyrol, see p102). Nhow's bar, restaurant, terrace and spa are all welcome additions to the area and, during the fair season, the hotel lets some of its spaces for photo shoots, exhibitions and fashion shows.
Via Tortona 35, T 02 7780 7229, www.nhow-hotels.com

Foresteria Monforte

'*Foresteria*' means guesthouse, and the Monforte offers three rooms – two standard and one suite – each done out in a contemporary style with a few antiques thrown in. There is no room service nor reception, yet this is a charming and highly affordable place to stay. The owners run the pharmacy downstairs and started to dabble in hospitality when they converted the first-floor apartment above the shop.

Each of the rooms has an LCD screen, high-speed internet connection and air-conditioning, and there's a communal kitchen where guests can prepare refreshments; garage parking is available on request. Well located (it's five minutes' walk to Piazza San Babila), the Monforte fills up fast, so book well in advance. *Piazza del Tricolore 2, T 02 7631 8516, www.foresteriamonforte.it*

Town House Galleria

The newest of Milan's three Town House hotels is located on the second and third floors of the Galleria, above Prada's store (see p086) and features 26 suites, butler service and a Bentley as house car. The 17-room Town House 31 (T 02 70 156) occupies a 19th-century *palazzina* on Via Goldoni and has a tented courtyard that serves as a bar in the summer. The Town House 12 hotel (T 02 8907 8511) is well situated for the fairs in the old Fiera Milano City exhibition centre, (not to be confused with the new Fiera Milano trade-fair complex, see p065), designed by Massimiliano Fuksas.
Via Silvio Pellico 8, www.townhouse.it

Hotel Principe di Savoia Milano

The Principe first opened its doors in 1927, and in 1938 was taken over by Ciga Hotels. Now operated by the Dorchester Group, it has 401 rooms decorated in classic Liberty style. The junior suites are in the adjoining tower (once the Duca Hotel), which is quite a trek from the front desk, so opt for a room in the original building (you'll wait less time for room service too). The hotel's Club 10 fitness and beauty centre has a rooftop terrace and is a good place to grab a *lettino* (sun lounger) and catch some rays; the indoor pool is just inside, along with a gym and a small spa. Under the glass ceiling of the hotel's Giardino d'Inverno Bar, with its over-the-top marble decor, there is a bit of a late-night drinking scene during Fashion Week. *Piazza della Repubblica 17, T 02 62 301, www.hotelprincipedisavoia.com*

Presidential Suite Pool, Hotel Principe di Savoia

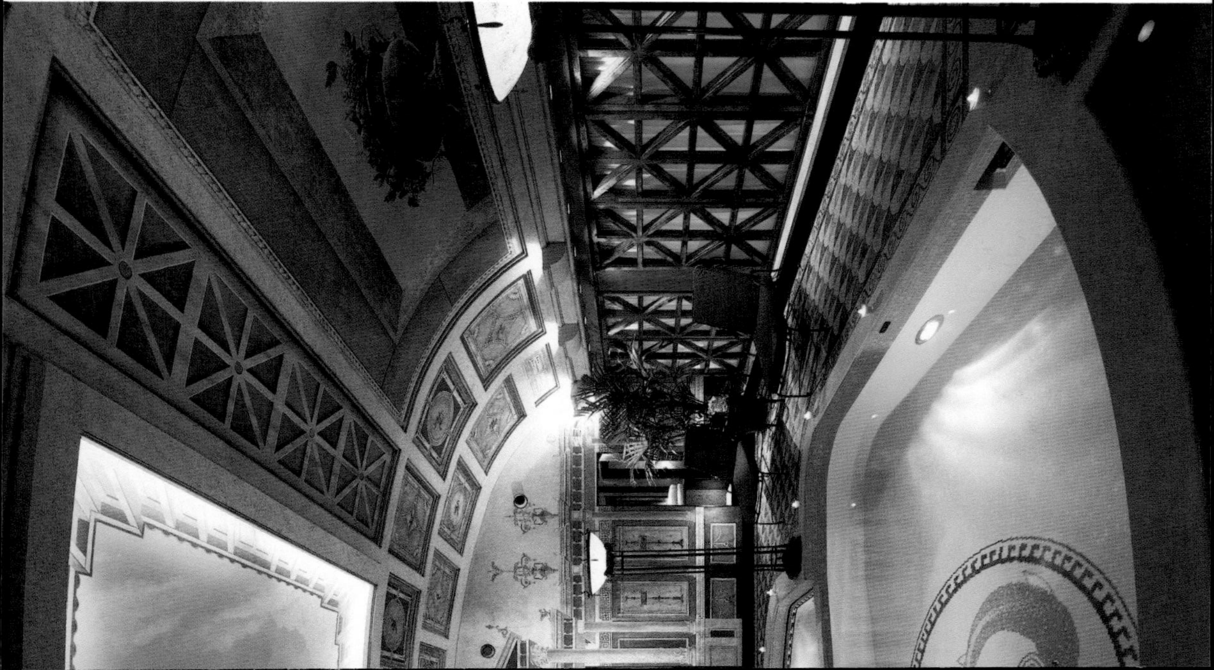

24 HOURS
SEE THE BEST OF THE CITY IN JUST ONE DAY

Our seven-step designer tour offers a more culturally demanding alternative to what has traditionally been our favourite pastime in Milan: trawling the boutiques along Via Montenapoleone, Via Sant'Andrea and Via della Spiga. After a *caffè* and brioche at Pasticceria Marchesi (Via Santa Maria alla Porta 11a, T 02 876 730), begin at the magical Museo Achille Castiglioni (opposite), which opened in 2006 in the studio where the late maestro of contemporary design worked for 40 years. Then move on to the Milan Triennale (Viale Alemagna 6, T 02 724 341), to take a look at their permanent collection of Italian design and any current exhibitions. Afterwards, stroll next door to Gio Ponti's Torre Branca (see p012), which reopened in 2003 after years of closure.

Before a lunch of focaccia at Princi (see p044), it's on to see the work of BBPR, Gio Pomodoro and Lucio Fontana at the Cimitero Monumentale (see p042). After lunch, head to some of Milan's best new galleries, where you can buy original works. If you have time, check out an exhibition at the Prada Foundation (Via Antonio Fogazzaro 36, T 02 5467 0515), but call ahead first, as they hold only a few shows a year. Then bid farewell to designers and say hello to another much-loved Milan institution – the sun lamp – at the Rino Beauty Sun Center (Via Montenapoleone 25, T 02 7600 0945), so you can pass for a true Milanese on your night out. *For all addresses, see Resources.*

10.00 Studio Museo Achille Castiglioni

This museum is situated in the Milan studio where Achille Castiglioni worked until his death in 2002. Visitors can gain a unique insight into the outstanding career and rich legacy of one of Italy's most highly respected design talents, as the museum grants a rare opportunity to view the process behind Castiglioni's art. Marvel at his collection of everyday objects, his 'tools of design instruction', some of which inspired his greatest projects, and the vast number of sketches, photographs, prototypes and objects that he produced. The museum is open on weekday mornings only.
Piazza Castello 27, T 02 805 3606,
for appointments

12.00 Cimitero Monumentale

This grand cemetery, which opened in 1866, is filled with a fascinating array of contemporary and classical Italian sculpture, as well as temples and obelisks. We suggest you seek out the post-war tombs and monuments designed by some of Italy's leading architects and sculptors.
Piazzale Cimitero Monumentale,
T 02 8846 5600

13.30 Princi

In the morning, locals arrive at this bakery, which was designed by Claudio Silvestrin, for their *caffè* and brioche. You can reach it in time for lunch by taking a stroll through Parco Sempione from the Torre Branca (see p012). On arrival, order *focaccia di Recco* (if it's still baking in the oven, be patient – it's well worth the wait) or a slice of freshly made pizza and then eat standing up, Milanese-style, while watching the Armani-clad bakers at work through a wall that is part glass and part rough porphyry stone. Princi has five locations in the city, and stays open until the evening for *aperitivi*.
Piazza XXV Aprile 5, T 02 2906 0832, www.princi.it

15.30 Tingo Design Gallery
Not far from the cemetery is Via Volta, where you should visit Tingo Design Gallery, the place to pick up pieces by Ugo La Pietra and Angelo Mangiarotti. Nearby is Via Maroncelli, where you will find Galleria MK (see p076), our favoured location for buying post-war Italian glass and lighting.
Via Alessandro Volta 18, T 02 2901 7239, www.tingo.it

URBAN LIFE
CAFÉS, RESTAURANTS, BARS AND NIGHTCLUBS

Milan has some fine *pasticcerie* that double up as cafés in which you can enjoy the city's favourite hot drink, *caffè*. Breakfast is usually a cappuccino and a brioche taken standing up at the bar. Tea is a little more complicated, as it seems not one *barista* in Milan realises that you need boiling water to make it properly. Avoid ordering a cappuccino after lunch, unless you want to be openly sneered at by the staff (it's strictly *macchiato* from midday on).

If you don't have time for a long lunch, it's a good idea to visit one of the many bakers in the city and fill up on focaccia or pizza by the slice. The branch of Princi located on Piazza XXV Aprile 5 (see p044) is an excellent choice. When dining, you can't go wrong with sumptuous stalwarts such as Bice (Via Borgospesso 12, T 02 7600 2572), Da Giacomo (Via Pasquale Sottocorno 6, T 02 7602 3313) or Le Langhe (Corso Como 6, T 02 655 4279). You can also enjoy great food in traditional restaurants, where the decor hasn't changed in years, although the lighting tends to be of the fluorescent variety. For some reason, many of the city's new eateries just don't seem to get the food right, even if the interiors look good and the lighting is better. The restaurant at the Bulgari Hotel (see p017) is an exception, however. Early evening is *aperitivo* time. The Italians are light drinkers and nurse their cocktails while nibbling a selection of complimentary snacks.

For all addresses, see Resources.

Pasticceria Cucchi

Cucchi has stood on the corner of Corso Genova and Piazza Resistenza Partigiana since 1936, and the place is still run by the Cucchi family. Pop in for a coffee at the bar (pay first at the till); or if you want to enjoy a more leisurely visit, settle yourself at a table outside, under the trees. Just remember the 'no cappuccino after lunch' protocol. Everything is made on the premises, and the *sfoglie con la mela* (apple pasties) are particularly good. Cucchi is open from 7am until 10pm every day except Monday.
Corso Genova 1, T 02 8940 9793

Gucci Caffè

Recently joining Prada (see p086), which first opened its doors in 1913, in the Galleria Vittorio Emanuele II (see p013) are Tod's, Louis Vuitton, Church's Shoes and Gucci. This is Gucci's second store in Milan, selling accessories (the Via Montenapoleone store has more merchandise), but it's the first Gucci boutique in the world with its own café. And the café makes a refreshing change from others in the Galleria, which tend to be overpriced tourist traps. Coffee or tea is served with chocolates that are created by pastry chef Ernst Knam and decorated with the brand's logo. The Gucci Caffè is closed on Sunday mornings.
Galleria Vittorio Emanuele II, T 02 859 7991

Osteria La Carbonaia Mare

La Carbonaia Mare serves only seafood. The interior design is amusing, with small portholes on the walls, and has not been updated much since 1979 – although the charming blue chairs are on their last legs and may be replaced soon. The best thing is to forget about the menu entirely and ask the waiter to bring an assortment of dishes. For *antipasti*, request a selection of seafood salads, such as prawns with artichokes, or octopus with potato, or choose one of the marinated raw fish dishes. For your main course, you can't go wrong with *branzino al sale* (sea bass cooked in salt), and make sure you order the courgette chips.

Via San Vittore/Via Giosué Carducci,
T 02 4800 4638

Armani Nobu and Armani Privé

Milan is the epicentre of Giorgio Armani's empire. In addition to buying his clothing, accessories, beauty and homewares, you can stop off at the Armani Caffè (T 02 6231 2680) or dine at Armani Nobu, which serves Nobuyuki Matsuhisa's famed Japanese cuisine. You'll also find a bar for drinks and light dining inside Armani Nobu. After dinner, head downstairs to Armani Privé (open 11pm to 3am). Diners benefit from internal access, while others must enter from the street and may have to queue. This is a good spot for people spotting, particularly if you want to check out local footballers and visiting celebs. *Armani Nobu, Via Gastone Pisoni 1, T 02 6231 2645; Armani Privé, Via Alessandro Manzoni 31, T 02 6231 2655*

Martini Bar

Fed up with not having a good place
to meet and drink in central Milan, fashion
designers Domenico Dolce and Stefano
Gabbana decided to open their own place.
The Martini Bar is set within a courtyard
behind their impressive David Chipperfield
and Ferruccio Laviani-designed men's
store. The circular space has a black
mosaic floor complete with a red dragon,
curved banquettes, black leather pouffes
and chrome and glass cocktail tables.
The courtyard, with citrus trees, is the
place to hang out in the summer. A wide
range of cocktails is on offer, served by
Dolce & Gabbana-clad waiters. While you
are there, check out the Barbiere (see
p093) and the Beauty Farm (see p092).
Corso Venezia 15, T 02 7601 1154

Moscatelli

Moscatelli calls itself a *bottiglieria*, which means 'wine shop', but this place is more of an *enoteca* or wine bar, and has been open since 1859. Come for a lunch of fresh pasta, risotto or a simple meat dish. In the early evening, you should sample the fabulous Italian wines on offer, by the glass or bottle, accompanied by a plate or two of meats, such as *prosciutto di Parma*, *coppa piacentina*, *lardo di colonnato* or *mortadella di tartufo*, or opt for cheeses served with honey. You may not need any dinner afterwards. Moscatelli is open until midnight from Monday to Saturday, but is closed on Sunday.
Corso Garibaldi 93, T 02 655 4602

Da Giordano Il Bolognese
We love the 1950s decor and classic
Bolognese food served here. Grilled
vegetables make a good *antipasto*,
along with mixed salami, followed by
home-made pasta. On Friday, there is
fish on the menu and, once a week, you
can order *bollito misto* (mixed boiled
meats) served with *mostarda*.
Corso Genova 3 (entrance on Via Torti),
T 02 5810 0824

Alla Collina Pistoiese

The cuisine here is Tuscan, which means crostini, soups, pasta and lots of meat. The *costata alla fiorentina* (T-bone steak) is one of the restaurant's most popular dishes and the grilled fish is also good. In summer, it's worth ordering *prosciutto* with figs, and in winter the *insalata di carciofi* (baby artichoke salad with Parmesan and celery). The restaurant's decor has not changed much since 1938, when it was opened by Pietro Gori. Today, it's run by the third and fourth generations of the same family.
Via Amedei 1, T 02 8645 1085

Obikà

Think of a sushi bar, substitute raw fish for mozzarella, and you have the concept behind Obikà, Milan's first mozzarella bar. It serves *mozzarella di bufala* from Campania, freshness guaranteed as the buffalo are milked in the morning, the cheese produced in the afternoon, and it arrives in Milan early the next day. In addition to the four varieties of mozzarella on offer (try them all), Obikà sells specialities from artisanal producers all over Italy, including the delicious *burrata* from Andria in Puglia, and *nduja di Spezzano Picolo*, a spreadable salami from Calabria. This is a great place for an *aperitivo*.
*Via Mercato 28, T 02 8645 0568,
www.obika.it*

Il Baretto al Baglioni
Although, truthfully, we preferred its
original location, Il Baretto, now housed
inside the Baglioni Hotel, remains a
favourite choice for lunch (when the
clientele is mostly made up of the CEOs
of top design houses), dinner or just
an après-shopping *aperitivo*. Those
in the know use the back door on Via
Della Spiga 6.
Via Senato 7, T 02 781 255

INSIDER'S GUIDE
ANTONIA GIACINTI, BOUTIQUE OWNER

Antonia Giacinti heads up the eponymous Antonia boutiques (see p084), which stock all the clothes and accessories that Giacinti would include in her ideal wardrobe, such as French brands Balenciaga, Chloé, Lanvin and Pierre Hardy, and the chic Italian labels Dolce & Gabbana, Bottega Veneta and Haute by Vincenzo di Cotiis (who originally designed her stores and windows).

To navigate Milan, Giacinti recommends getting about by scooter (you can rent one from Bianco Blu, Via Gallarate 33, T 02 308 2430). For breakfast, she stops at Pasticceria Marchesi (Via Santa Maria alla Porta 11a, T 02 876 730), where she eats standing up at the bar (there are no tables). After work, it's *aperitivo* time at the Bulgari Hotel (see p017); in summer, you'll find her in the garden or on the terrace. If not at the Bulgari, Giacinti heads to La Cantina di Manuela (Via Raffaello Sanzio 16, T 02 4398 3048) – an *enoteca* with several branches in the city – for a glass of red wine and a plate of cheeses served with honey or cured meats. For dinner, Giacinti often stays on at the Bulgari Hotel, or she likes to visit the Japanese-style restaurant Fingers (Via San Gerolamo Emiliani 2, T 02 5412 2675) for sushi ('It's full of my clients, but they are all friends too'), or the tiny Latteria (Via San Marco 24, T 02 659 7653), which serves the kind of simple Italian food that she prefers to eat at home.

For all addresses, see Resources.

ARCHITOUR

A GUIDE TO MILAN'S ICONIC BUILDINGS

It should be said that Milan is not the first port of call for the veteran Italian architourist. The Duomo (see p014), which took more than 400 years to complete and, as a result, runs the gamut of architectural expression, from gothic to baroque and renaissance, is still the primary draw. Aside from that, Milan's architectural pleasures are rather understated – a rationalist villa here, a modernist housing complex there, sandwiched between acres of samey social housing and public buildings.

Milan's architectural hero is undoubtedly Gio Ponti, whose elegant Pirelli Tower (see p010) is still the most potent symbol of the city. Recently refurbished, its sleek form minimises the effect such a tall tower has on a dense, millennia-old city plan. Ponti's influence overshadowed all areas of Milan's creative life, from publishing to architecture to product design and even to sets for La Scala opera house (Piazza della Scala, T 02 88 791). Contemporary architecture is rare indeed, with the exception of Tadao Ando's Teatro Armani (see p066) and Massimiliano Fuksas' bold new trade fair Fiera Milano (right). This is about to change for the better, as the recent completion of the latter is making way for 'City Life', an ambitious multi-use redevelopment project with towers and buildings by Arata Isozaki, Daniel Libeskind, Zaha Hadid and Pier Paolo Maggiora, due for completion by 2016.

For all addresses, see Resources.

Fiera Milano

Just outside Milan, in Rho-Pero (a 40-minute subway ride away), on the reclaimed site of an oil refinery, stands Massimiliano Fuksas' new trade fair complex. Its central element is a glass and steel structure that runs like a giant ribbon caressing the large and small scale buildings along its path (an impressive 1.5km) and ends in a huge crater-like vortex at either end. Nicknamed *La Vela*, 'The Sail', by an enthusiastic Italian media even before completion, it covers a raised walkway, flanked on either side by four giant exhibition halls and a variety of smaller structures containing bars, restaurants and shops.
Strada Statale del Sempione 28, T 02 49 971, www.nuovosistemafieramilano.it

Teatro Armani

Giorgio Armani's worldwide commercial headquarters occupy what was once a Nestlé factory, masterfully transformed by Japanese architect Tadao Ando. The 12,000 sq m site includes offices, showrooms, a dining room, a reflecting pool and a 3,400 sq m multifunctional theatre. It's here that Armani presents his fashion shows and home collections. *Via Bergognone 59*

Villa Figini

Built in 1935, this is one of the first examples of rationalist architecture in Italy. The architect Luigi Figini claimed the house was inspired by the Villa Savoye, which is just outside Paris (T 00 33 1 3965 0106), and he was part of a small group of Italians influenced more by the new Europeans Mies Van der Rohe and Le Corbusier, who designed the Villa Savoye, than the local ideology. Rigorous, with its simple volumes, the house stands on 12 pillars, leaving the garden almost completely intact beneath, aside from the staircase. The first floor reveals an interior patio behind the front shutter, and the second-floor terrace includes a marble-clad pool at the back.
Via Ettore Perrone di San Martino 8

Corso Italia Complex

One of Luigi Moretti's few Milanese buildings, the dense arrangement of apartments, shops, offices and a garage was completed in 1953. The Roman architect and urbanist was also responsible for the Watergate centre in Washington, his only project in the US, and, like Gio Ponti, edited his own magazine, *Space*. In this complex of buildings, Moretti carried forward the themes of volume and plasticism that he had already developed in previous projects. The main component, an undulating nine-storey office slab, which reaches out dramatically over the street, seems to cut through the three-storey structure below. The awkwardly shaped site and its various functions make for a remarkable building.
Corso Italia 13-17

Chiesa di San Francesco
Gio Ponti's Pirelli Tower (see p010) may be his best known and most visible office building in the city where he was based, but the architect was prolific in Milan and produced, among other things, this remarkable church in 1964. Built with Antonio Fornaroli and Laberto Roselli, the facade is clad almost entirely in diamond-shaped tiles.
Via Paolo Giovio 41

SHOPPING

THE CITY'S BEST SHOPS AND WHAT TO BUY

Milan's major attraction is its shopping and, in particular, the 'Golden Triangle' of Via Montenapoleone, Via della Spiga and Via Sant'Andrea. Fendi (Via Sant'Andrea 16, T 02 7602 1617), Gucci (Via Montenapoleone 5 and 7, T 02 771 271), Prada (see p086), Missoni (Via Sant'Andrea/Via Bagutta T 02 7600 3555), Giorgio Armani (Via Sant'Andrea 9, T 02 7600 3234) and Valentino (Via Montenapoleone 20, T 02 7600 5242) are all here. The area has recently opened up, and now incorporates Corso Venezia, where you can stock up on Miu Miu (number 3, T 02 7600 1799) and Dolce & Gabbana (number 15, T 02 778 831).

Head to Carshoe (Via della Spiga 50, T 02 7602 4027) if you want great driving shoes. For bespoke suits, make an appointment at Brioni (Via Gesù 3, T 02 7639 0086), where you can also check out the women's ready-to-wear range by Cristina Ortiz. Valextra (see p085) has superb small leather goods, briefcases and luggage. Source pecorino, Parmesan, prosciutto and other culinary delicacies from the best Italian artisan producers at Derè (Via Mercato 20, T 02 8691 5224). Via Durini specialises in furniture from the likes of B&B Italia (Via Durini 14, T 02 764 441), while Via Brera is home to a charming selection of shops, such as Anna Maria Consadori Gallery (number 2, T 02 7202 1767), which stocks 1950s paintings by Roberto Crippa and Lucio Fontana busts.

For all addresses, see Resources.

Viktor & Rolf

Dutch mavericks Viktor Horsting and Rolf Snoeren chose Milan as the location for their first store. The shop, like their collection, is classic with quite a twist. Architect Siebe Tettero, together with Sherrie Zwail of SZI Design, revisited 18th-century Dutch and Swedish neoclassicism when they created the space. The twist? Every detail is upside down, so the oak parquet flooring is on the ceiling, from which hang grey chairs that flank fireplaces, while crystal chandeliers spring from the floor. The entire collection of women's ready-to-wear clothing, shoes and the 'Flowerbomb' fragrance, as well as the duo's charmingly named menswear, Viktor & Rolf Monsieur, is available here. *Via Sant'Andrea 14, T 02 796 091, www.viktor-rolf.com*

Viktor & Rolf

Galleria MK

Via Pietro Maroncelli, a short walk from Corso Como, is home to several new and interesting galleries, including Galleria MK, where we spotted this unique 1960s lamp (above) by Barbini, a glass-maker from Murano. Other Milan Galleries have been known to source from MK, which surely means that the merchandise and the prices are too tempting even for them. This is one of our favourite locations for collectable glass, lamps, objects and furniture. Just a few doors up the road, at number 10, is Galleria Rossella Colombari, (T 02 2900 1189) – the place to head for Carlo Mollino's divine furniture.

Via Pietro Maroncelli 2, T 02 655 1035

Danese

As the original store shut down about 20 years ago, we were the first in line when Danese reopened in Milan a couple of years ago. This is the place to pick up desirable objects, such as Bruno Munari's 1964 'Falkland' lamp, or Enzo Mari's 'Canarie' desk set from 1958 and 'Formosa' calendar from 1963. Newly reissued items include this 'Putrella' dish (above), €434, also by Mari, first produced in 1958. Danese has recently uncovered a small amount of original stock no longer in production, such as Mari's 'Tongavera' bowls and 'Living' books. If ever there was a genuine 'hurry while stocks last' moment, this is it. *Piazza San Nazaro in Brolo 15, T 02 5830 4150, www.danesemilano.com*

Lula Cioccolato

When not engaged in his day job designing womenswear (he is half of the team behind the recently relaunched Ken Scott label), Lula's Antonio Ponte scours Italy and France for *artigianale* (artisan) chocolates. Lula also makes its own, in delightful flavours such as saffron, rose water, and tonka bean with apricot. This tiny store in Milan's Cinque Giornata area is a visual feast, too, with its vintage fittings and signature floral wallpaper. The packaging is almost as delicious: some boxes are covered in vintage fabrics that Ponte collects on his travels. It is hard to leave empty-handed.
Via Archimede/Via Fiamma 17,
T 02 7000 6915, www.lulamilano.com

Poltrona Frau

Milan was Gio Ponti's base, so take a small piece of him home with this 'Dezza' chair (above), €1,900 (a two-seater is also available), created in 1965 and recently put back into production. According to historical notes, it was designed to be 'lightweight, adaptable and easy to take down, to be shipped anywhere', so there is no excuse. Poltrona Frau has a few other gems in its back catalogue, such as the 'Sanluca' armchair by Achille Castiglioni and his brother, Pier Giacomo (the original sits in Castiglioni's museum, see p041). For those who are looking for something more recent, Jean-Marie Massaud has designed the fine 'Don'Do' rocking chair; the Frenchman was also responsible for the new store design. *Via della Moscova 58, T 02 657 1205, www.poltronafrau.it*

Aspesi

Alberto Aspesi's range of chic sportswear, cut from the best Italian and Japanese fabrics, is a Milan institution, but a well-guarded secret elsewhere. That's all about to change, as he has recently opened his first dedicated store in the city. Spanning two streets, with entrances on both Via Bigli and Via Montenapoleone, and boasting a courtyard and a café, the store is designed by Antonio Citterio (who also built Aspesi's factory), along with Dirk Van Dooren from design collective Tomato. The signature nylon outerwear, called *piumini*, is functional, stylish and comes in an array of colours. The range includes this padded shirt (above), €164. Lawrence Steele designs the popular womenswear.
*Via Montenapoleone 13 and Via Bigli 4,
T 02 861 792, www.aspesi.it*

Laura Urbinati

While Milan's shopping scene is crowded with international brand names you probably already know, it's worth checking out some other stores with niche products. Milan-based designer Laura Urbinati has just three shops, in Rome, Los Angeles and Milan. She designs and produces her own line, which includes not only rather nice lingerie but exceedingly well-cut swimwear, cover-ups and easy separates.

Great fit and shapes as well as colour and print are her forte, and this tiny store in the Ticinese neighbourhood is a treasure trove well worth a visit. Bras start at €70 and knickers at €50. *Piazza San Eustorgio 6, T 02 836 0411, www.lauraurbinati.com*

È De Padova
De Padova produces and distributes furniture and products by some of the greats of Italian design, such as Achille Castiglioni, Pierluigi Cerri and Vico Magistretti, as well as works by emerging talents, including the Belgian Xavier Lust and the Japanese firms Setsu e Shinobu ITO and Nendo. Maddalena De Padova's beautiful store on the corner of Corso Venezia and Via Senato opened 41 years ago and has introduced innovative ideas and products to the city ever since. Making full use of her giant windows, she often had Castiglioni in to design the *allestimento* (display). De Padova recently purchased the whole building, gaining an additional two floors (there are now six in total) and making her showroom space probably the largest and most stunning in Milan.
Corso Venezia 14, T 02 777 201,
www.depadova.it

Antonia

In a city dominated by *mono-mark* stores, Antonia and its sister retail outlet Antonia Accessori are rare breeds indeed for Milan. The stores and displays have been designed by Vincenzo de Cotiis – also responsible for the edgy Hotel Straf (see p026) and the fashion label Haute – while the merchandise is selected by owner Antonia Giacinti (see p062) to provide the components of the perfect wardrobe.

Clothing is from brands such as Lanvin, Balenciaga, Chloé, Dolce & Gabbana, Fendi and Haute. Next door, drool over accessories by the likes of Marc Jacobs, Renè Caovilla, Christian Louboutin, Bruno Frisoni and Gucci. It's always worth checking out the new names in store, too. *Via Ponte Vetero 1, T 02 869 0216*

Valextra

The name Valextra is derived from *valigia* (suitcase) and *extra* (first class), and this store is the place to head when looking for the best travel goods. Its range includes some great *prodotti storici* (historical products), which were first created by founder Giovanni Fontana in the 1940s, as well as new lines. Valextra specialises in luggage (of the not-to-be-checked-in variety) as well as small leather goods (made in 'VL' grained calfskin) that are so more-ish you can easily become a collector. Take home its superb travel wallet with a slot to slip in your passport in its matching cover. Or invest in the perfect travel bag (above), €2,144.
*Via Alessandro Manzoni 3,
T 02 9978 6000, www.valextra.com*

Prada

This is where it all began: the original Prada store, opened in Galleria Vittorio Emanuele II in 1913 by Miuccia Prada's grandfather, Mario Prada. Although subtly enlarged recently, its Belgium marble chequered floor and mahogany and brass furniture are all original. There are now an additional five Prada stores in Milan: in Via Montenapoleone, there's menswear at number 6 (T 02 7602 0273), with women's ready-to-wear and accessories at number 8 (T 02 7777 1771); Via della Spiga now has a women's accessories store at number 18 (T 02 780 465) and women's lingerie at number 5 (T 02 7601 4448); while the branch at Via Sant'Andrea 21 (T 02 7600 1426) sells the sportier Linea Rossa Collection.

Galleria Vittorio Emanuele II,
T 02 876 979, www.prada.com

G Lorenzi

Long established as a master *coltellinaio*, or cutler (it first opened its doors in 1929), G Lorenzi now extends way beyond the traditional knives, cutlery and scissors. Head here for all you need to slice prosciutto, Parmesan and truffles, as well as to achieve grooming perfection with its impressive range of hand-made Madagascan ebony brushes (nail brush, above, €46), nail scissors, shoehorns, razors and mirrors. Ask to be shown one item on display, and get to see hundreds more locked away in drawers. Other treasures to be found here include a fabulous compact espresso-maker set, which plugs into a car dashboard (with international plugs for off-road use), and bamboo-handled picnic sets.
Via Montenapoleone 9, T 02 7602 2848, www.lorenzi.it

SPORTS AND SPAS
WORK OUT, CHILL OUT OR JUST WATCH

Milan's gym culture has improved recently. Gyms in the city would find it hard to compete with those in London, LA or New York; however, <u>Downtown</u> (Piazza Diaz 6, T 02 863 1181) and <u>Caroli Health Club</u> (Via Senato 11, T 02 7602 8517) cater to visitors.

Italian-style yoga would be unrecognisable to serious practitioners based elsewhere in the world, so it may be best to avoid it while visiting Milan. Joggers should head to Parco Sempione, behind <u>Castello Sforzesco</u> (Piazza Castello, T 02 8846 3700), or the Giardini Pubblici di Porta Venezia, although you may need to run round at least eight times to get a good workout. The emergence of spas in the last few years has brought a welcome addition to the city, but be warned, many massage technicians are very light in the touch (and by all accounts in their training, too). Milan's designers were the first to import the spa culture to the city. Gianfranco Ferré opened an <u>E'Spa</u> next to his boutique on Via Sant'Andrea 15 (T 02 7601 7526), overlooking a private garden, and Dolce & Gabbana has its <u>Beauty Farm</u> (see p092) set within a courtyard inside its men's store at Corso Venezia 15. This offers a complete range of body and beauty treatments in glorious, marble-clad surroundings. Its barbershop, <u>Barbiere</u> (see p093), offers a treat of its own, the Sicilian Wet Shave – taken on a period barber chair under a vintage Murano chandelier.

For all addresses, see Resources.

Bulgari Spa

The experience begins when you enter the blissful garden in which the spa sits, and leave behind any thoughts of being in the centre of Milan. Designed by Antonio Citterio and Partners, the treatment rooms and gym are sleekly fitted out in teak, bronze and stone. Arrive early to make use of the matt gold mosaic pool and Turkish bath (set within a brilliant emerald-glass cube). Guests get a spa cuisine lunch prepared by the hotel chef. Our favourite treatments utilise hot stone therapy, where heated smooth stones soaked in blended oils are placed on the body or used to gently massage pressure points. The holistic foot and nail treatment is the perfect antidote to Milan's cobbled streets. Open every day.
Via Privata Fratelli Gabba 7b, T 02 80 580 5200, www.bulgarihotels.com

Bulgari Spa

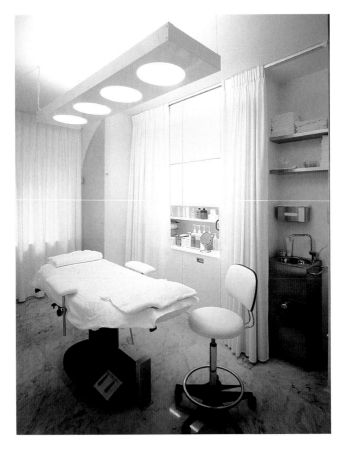

Dolce & Gabbana Beauty Farm

David Chipperfield and Ferruccio Laviani converted an 18th-century *palazzo* into a chic men's store for Dolce & Gabbana; and the fashion duo's Beauty Farm and Barbiere (a barbershop) is set behind this, within a courtyard. Beauty Farm (we preferred its original name, Grooming) offers a full range of body and beauty treatments, including massage, facials, manicures, pedicures and waxing for both male and female clients. The walls and floors are all white Carrara marble, with Knoll furniture. The feel is that of a stylish, modern Swiss clinic – Italian style.
Corso Venezia 15, T 02 7640 8888

Barbiere

Just across the citrus tree-lined courtyard from Beauty Farm is Barbiere, Dolce & Gabbana's barbershop. The green marble walls and warm chestnut cabinets give this all-male environment a traditional feel. In addition to a cut, wash and dry, Barbiere offers the Sicilian Wet Shave. The treatment includes being wrapped with piping hot towels and massaged with foaming creams before and after the shave with a cut-throat blade. It's a highly sensuous experience. Afterwards, retire to D&G's Martini Bar (see p054).
Corso Venezia 15, T 02 7640 8881

Habits Culti

In the chic Magenta neighbourhood, just off Corso Vercelli, is Habits Culti. Upstairs, browse through Alessandro Agrati's range of homewares, flowers, chocolates, panettone, tisanes and coffee, then head downstairs to the spa. In summer, try the ultimate hot-weather fix, Hammam Refreshing – a body scrub using a silk glove, followed by an application of clay lightly mixed with ice. Afterwards, a creamy Syrian olive-oil soap and essential oil is applied with one hand and ice lightly brushed over with the other. A minty mist shower, followed by a hot, then cold shower and steam is topped off by a massage. In winter, the same treatment is offered without the ice. When your treatment is finished, call into the adjoining café/restaurant Noy for a drink or a light snack; Noy is open every day.
Via Angelo Mauri 5, T 02 4851 7588,
www.habitsculti.it

ESCAPES

WHERE TO GO IF YOU WANT TO LEAVE TOWN

Most Milanese take advantage of the city's proximity to lakes, mountains and the coast; many of them spend practically every weekend away. The nearby lakes offer the quickest escape: Como is a mere 40 minutes away; as is Lugano, just inside the border with Switzerland; and it takes just over an hour to get to Desenzano, on Lake Garda. All can be reached easily by train from Milan Central Station (Piazza Duca d'Aosta, www.trenitalia.it).

For a swim in the sea, head for Santa Margherita or Portofino in Liguria; it's just over two hours on the train or by car. The place to stop is Paraggi, a little bay just before Portofino. Most beaches are private, so try Bagni Fiore (Via Paraggi a Mare 1, Santa Margherita Ligure, Paraggi, T 01 8528 4831) or Hotel Paraggi (Santa Margherita Ligure, Paraggi, T 01 8528 9961), where you can stay the night. Both serve simple Ligurian fare for lunch. Portofino is an upmarket fishing village, with impressive shopping and fine restaurants. Try Hotel San Giorgio (Via del Fondaco 11, Portofino, T 01 852 6991). If you have a few days, head to a mountain spa. Therme Vals (see p098) can be reached by car from Milan in about three and a half hours. The South Tyrol region offers two options: Vigilius Mountain Resort in Lana (see p102) or Terme Merano (opposite). To reach either, take a train from Milan's Central Station to Bolzano, and then a taxi (they are around 30km away).

For all addresses, see Resources.

Terme Merano

Merano is in the South Tyrol, at the basin of the Texal Mountains, and has a unique microclimate, 300 days a year of sunshine, and a brand-new thermal baths and hotel, designed by local architect Matteo Thun, who is a one-man wellness industry in the region (see p103). Spread over 7,500 sq m, facilities include 25 pools, inside under Thun's giant glass cube, and outside in the lush parklands. The vast sauna zone (mixed and swimwear-free) includes a sauna, two steam baths, a caldarium and a Finnish log-cabin sauna. There is a fitness centre, a medical centre and a Spa & Vitality centre with 30 specially designed rooms offering 'Altoatesini' treatments. Thun also designed the 139-room hotel with subterranean access to the Terme. *Piazza Terme 9, Merano, T 04 7325 2000, www.termemerano.it*

Therme Vals

Milan's closeness to the Swiss border means that Therme Vals is a pleasant car journey away. Here, Peter Zumthor has used 60,000 slabs of Valser quarzite to create a cathedral to bathing, with indoor and outdoor pools. The use of light and shade, and open and enclosed spaces, enhances the feeling of wellbeing, as you enjoy the health benefits of the local thermal spring water. Book well in advance for the wellness centre, which offers a wide range of treatments. Stay at the connecting Hotel Therme Vals (T 00 41 08 1926 8080), requesting one of the Zumthor-designed rooms, or at our favourite, the family guesthouse Hotel Alpina (00 41 08 1935 1148); be sure to ask for a modernised room.
Vals, Switzerland, T 00 41 08 1926 8008, www.therme-vals.ch

Alpine village of Vals

Vigilius Mountain Resort
Take a cable car to reach architect
Matteo Thun's Vigilius Mountain Resort,
which sits in sublime isolation 1,500m
high. The service doesn't always match
the surroundings, but the hay-bath cure,
a therapy practised in the Dolomites for
centuries, really does work wonders on
circulation complaints and cellulite.
*Vigiloch, Lana, South Tyrol, T 04 7355
6600, www.vigilius.com*

NOTES
SKETCHES AND MEMOS

RESOURCES

ADDRESSES AND ROOM RATES

LANDMARKS

009 Castello Sforzesco
Piazza Castello
T 02 8846 3700
www.milanocastello.it

009 Milan Triennale
Viale Alemagna 6
T 02 724 341
www.triennale.it

010 Pirelli Tower
Piazza Duca d'Aosta 3

011 Torre Velasca
Piazza Velasca 5

012 Torre Branca
Viale Luigi Camoen
Parco Sempione
T 02 331 4120

013 Galleria Vittorio Emanuele II
Piazza del Duomo/
Piazza della Scala

014 Duomo
Piazza del Duomo

HOTELS

017 Bulgari Hotel
Room rates:
double, €590-€650;
Executive Suite,
€1,200-€1,600
Via Privata Fratelli Gabba 7b
T 02 805 8051
www.bulgarihotels.com

020 Park Hyatt Milan
Room rates:
double, €430-€550;
Rooms 105 and 205, €725;
Diplomatic Suite, €3,000
Via Tommaso Grossi 1
T 02 8821 1234
www.milan.park.hyatt.com

020 La Scala
Piazza della Scala
T 02 88 791

024 Four Seasons
Room rates:
double, €725;
Suites 014, 016, 018
and 019, €1,850;
Cloister Suite 115, €2,400
Via Gesù 6-8
T 02 77 088
www.fourseasons.com/milan

026 Straf
Room rates:
double, €308;
Well-Being Room, €352
Via San Raffaele 3
T 02 805 081
www.straf.it

030 3Rooms
Room rates:
double, €310
Corso Como 10
T 02 626 163
www.3rooms-10corso como.com

030 10 Corso Como
Corso Como 10
T 02 2900 2674
www.10corso como.com

030 Colette
213 rue Saint-Honoré, 1e
Paris
France
T 00 33 1 5535 3390
www.colette.fr

032 Grand Hotel et de Milan
Room rates:
double, €544
Via Alessandro Manzoni 29
T 02 723 141
www.grandhotelet demilan.it

034 Nhow
Room rates on request
Via Tortona 35
T 02 7780 7229
www.nhow-hotels.com/
www.nh-hotels.com

035 Foresteria Monforte
Room rates:
double, €120
Piazza del Tricolore 2
T 02 7631 8516
www.foresteriamonforte.it

036 Town House Galleria
Room rates on request
Via Silvio Pellico 8
www.townhouse.it

036 Town House 12
Room rates:
double, €250-€390
Piazza Gerusalemme 12
T 02 8907 8511
www.townhouse.it

036 Town House 31
Room rates:
double, €250-€390
Via Goldoni 31
T 02 70 156
www.townhouse.it

037 Hotel Principe di Savoia Milano
Room rates:
double, €380;
Elegant Suite, €740;
Presidential Suite,
€13,000
Piazza della Repubblica 17
T 02 62 301
www.hotelprincipedi savoia.com

24 HOURS
040 Pasticceria Marchesi
Via Santa Maria alla Porta 11a
T 02 876 730

040 Prada Foundation
Via Antonio Fogazzaro 36
T 02 5467 0515
www.fondazioneprada.org

040 Rino Beauty Sun Center
Via Montenapoleone 25
T 02 7600 0945

041 Studio Museo Achille Castiglioni
Piazza Castello 27
T 02 805 3606

042 Cimitero Monumentale
Piazzale Cimitero Monumentale
T 02 8846 5600

044 Princi
Piazza XXV Aprile 5
T 02 2906 0832
www.princi.it

046 Tingo Design Gallery
Via Alessandro Volta 18
T 02 2901 7239
www.tingo.it

URBAN LIFE
048 Bice
Via Borgospesso 12
T 02 7600 2572
www.bicemilano.it

048 Da Giacomo
Via Pasquale Sottocorno 6
T 02 7602 3313

048 Le Langhe
Corso Como 6
T 02 655 4279

049 Pasticceria Cucchi
Corso Genova 1
T 02 8940 9793

050 Gucci Caffè
Galleria Vittorio Emanuele II
T 02 859 7991

052 Osteria La Carbonaia Mare
Via San Vittore/Via Giosué Carducci
T 02 4800 4638

053 Armani Nobu
Via Gastone Pisoni 1
T 02 6231 2645
www.nobumatsuhisa.com

053 Armani Privé
Via Alessandro Manzoni 31
T 02 6231 2655

053 Armani Caffè
Via Alessandro Manzoni 31
T 02 6231 2680

054 Martini Bar
Corso Venezia 15
T 02 7601 1154

055 Moscatelli
Corso Garibaldi 93
T 02 655 4602

056 Da Giordano Il Bolognese
Corso Genova 3 (entrance on Via Torti)
T 02 5810 0824

058 Alla Collina Pistoiese
Via Amedei 1
T 02 8645 1085

059 Obikà
Via Mercato 28
T 02 8645 0568
www.obika.it

060 Il Baretto al Baglioni
Via Senato 7
T 02 781 255

062 Bianco Blu
Via Gallarate 33
T 02 308 2430
www.biancoblu.com
062 La Cantina di Manuela
Via Raffaello Sanzio 16
T 02 4398 3048
062 Fingers
Via San Gerolamo Emiliani 2
T 02 5412 2675
062 Latteria
Via San Marco 24
T 02 659 7653

ARCHITOUR
064 La Scala
Piazza della Scala
T 02 88 791
www.teatroallascala.org
065 Fiera Milano
Strada Statale del Sempione 28
T 02 49 971
www.nuovosistema fieramilano.it
066 Teatro Armani
Via Borgognone 59
068 Villa Figini
Via Ettore Perrone di San Martino 8
068 Villa Savoye
82 rue de Villiers
Poissy
France
T 00 33 1 3965 0106

069 Corso Italia Complex
Corso Italia 13-17
070 Chiesa di San Francesco
Via Paolo Giovio 41

SHOPPING
072 Anna Maria Consadori Gallery
Via Brera 2
T 02 7202 1767
072 B&B Italia
Via Durini 14
T 02 764 441
www.bebitalia.it
072 Brioni
Via Gesù 3
T 02 7639 0086
www.brioni.it
072 Carshoe
Via della Spiga 50
T 02 7602 4027
072 Derè
Via Mercato 20
T 02 8691 5224
072 Dolce & Gabbana
Corso Venezia 15
T 02 778 831
www.dolcegabbana.it
072 Fendi
Via Sant'Andrea 16
T 02 7602 1617
www.fendi.com
072 Giorgio Armani
Via Sant'Andrea 9
T 02 7600 3234

www.giorgioarmani.com
072 Gucci
Via Montenapoleone 5 and 7
T 02 771 271
www.gucci.com
072 Missoni
Via Sant'Andrea/Via Bagutta
T 02 7600 3555
www.missoni.com
072 Miu Miu
Corso Venezia 3
T 02 7600 1799
www.miumiu.com
072 Valentino
Via Montenapoleone 20
T 02 7600 5242
www.valentino.com
073 Viktor & Rolf
Via Sant'Andrea 14
T 02 796 091
www.viktor-rolf.com
076 Galleria MK
Via Pietro Maroncelli 2
T 02 655 1035
076 Galleria Rossella Colombari
Via Pietro Maroncelli 10
T 02 2900 1189
077 Danese
Piazza San Nazaro in Brolo 15
T 02 5830 4150
www.danesemilano.com
078 Lula Cioccolato
Via Archimede/Via Fiamma 17
T 02 7000 6915
www.lulamilano.com

079 Poltrona Frau
Via della Moscova 58
T 02 657 1205
www.poltronafrau.it
080 Aspesi
Via Montenapoleone 13
and Via Bigli 4
T 02 861 792
www.aspesi.it
081 Laura Urbinati
Piazza San Eustorgio 6
Milan
T 02 836 0411
Via dei Banchi Vecchi 50a
Rome
T 06 6813 6478
8667 Sunset Boulevard
Los Angeles
USA
T 001 310 652 3183
www.lauraurbinati.com
082 È De Padova
Corso Venezia 14
T 02 777 201
www.depadova.com
084 Antonia
Via Ponte Vetero 1
T 02 869 0216
085 Valextra
Via Alessandro Manzoni 3
T 02 9978 6000
www.valextra.com
086 Prada
Galleria Vittorio
Emanuele 11
T 02 876 979
Accessories
Via della Spiga 18
T 02 780 465

Linea Rossa
Via Sant'Andrea 21
T 02 7600 1426
Lingerie
Via della Spiga 5
T 02 7601 4448
Menswear
Via Montenapoleone 6
T 02 7602 0273
Womenswear
Via Montenapoleone 8
T 02 7777 1771
www.prada.com
087 G Lorenzi
Via Montenapoleone 9
T 02 7602 2848
www.lorenzi.it

SPORTS AND SPAS
088 Downtown
Piazza Diaz 6
T 02 863 1181
www.downtown
palestre.com
088 Caroli Health Club
Via Senato 11
T 02 7602 8517
www.carolihealthclub.it
088 E'Spa at Gianfranco Ferré
Via Sant'Andrea 15
T 02 7601 7526
www.gianfrancoferre.com
089 Bulgari Spa
Bulgari Hotel
Via Privata Fratelli
Gabba 7b
T 02 80 580 5200
www.bulgarihotel.com

092 Dolce & Gabbana Beauty Farm
Corso Venezia 15
T 02 7640 8888
093 Barbiere
Corso Venezia 15
T 02 7640 8881
095 Habits Culti Spa
Via Angelo Mauri 5
T 02 4851 7588
www.habitsculti.it
095 Noy
Via Angelo Mauri 5
T 02 4851 7286
www.habitsculti.it

ESCAPES
096 Bagni Fiore
Via Paraggi a Mare 1
Santa Margherita Ligure
Paraggi
T 01 8528 4831
www.bagnifiore.it
096 Hotel Paraggi
Santa Margherita Ligure
Paraggi
T 01 8528 9961
www.hotelparaggi.it
096 Hotel San Giorgio
Via del Fondaco 11
Portofino
T 01 852 6991
096 Milan Central Station
Piazza Duca d'Aosta
www.trenitalia.it

097 Terme Merano
Piazza Terme 9
Merano
T 04 7325 2000
098 Therme Vals
Hotel Therme
Vals
Switzerland
T 00 41 08 1926 8008
www.therme-vals.ch
098 Hotel Alpina
Vals
Switzerland
T 00 41 08 1935 1148
098 Hotel Therme
Vals
Switzerland
T 00 41 08 1926 8080
www.therme-vals.ch
102 Vigilius Mountain Resort
Vigiloch, Lana
South Tyrol
T 04 7355 6600
www.vigilius.com

WALLPAPER* CITY GUIDES

Editorial Director
Richard Cook

Art Director
Loran Stosskopf
City Editor
Nick Vinson
Series Editor
Jeroen Bergmans
Project Editor
Rachael Moloney
**Executive
Managing Editor**
Jessica Firmin

Chief Designer
Ben Blossom
Designers
Dominic Bell
Sara Martin
Ingvild Sandal
Map Illustrator
Russell Bell

Photography Editor
Emma Blau
Photography Assistant
Jasmine Labeau

Sub-Editor
Paul Sentobe
Editorial Assistant
Milly Nolan

**Wallpaper* Group
Editor-in-Chief**
Jeremy Langmead
Creative Director
Tony Chambers
Publishing Director
Fiona Dent

Thanks to
Paul Barnes
David McKendrick
Meirion Pritchard

PHAIDON

Phaidon Press Limited
Regent's Wharf
All Saints Street
London N1 9PA

Phaidon Press Inc
180 Varick Street
New York, NY 10014

www.phaidon.com

First published 2006
© 2006 Phaidon Press
Limited

ISBN 0 7148 4691 0

A CIP Catalogue record for
this book is available from
the British Library.

All prices are correct at
time of going to press, but
are subject to change.

Printed in China